I0025910

Debating Alternative Facts

The Elements of Debating and
How to Counter Arguments
with Ease Using Logic

Copyright © 2017 Reina Donovan

All rights reserved.

ISBN: 9780998793672

© Copyright 2017 by Tru Nobilis Publishing- All rights reserved.

The following eBook is reproduced below with the goal of providing information that is as accurate and as reliable as possible. Regardless, purchasing this eBook can be seen as consent to the fact that both the publisher and the author of this book are in no way experts on the topics discussed within, and that any recommendations or suggestions made herein are for entertainment purposes only. Professionals should be consulted as needed before undertaking any of the action endorsed herein.

This declaration is deemed fair and valid by both the American Bar Association and the Committee of Publishers Association and is legally binding throughout the United States.

Furthermore, the transmission, duplication or reproduction of any of the following work, including precise information, will be considered an illegal act, irrespective whether it is done electronically or in print. The legality extends to creating a secondary or tertiary copy of the work or a recorded copy and is only allowed with express written consent of the Publisher. All additional rights are reserved.

The information in the following pages is broadly considered to be a truthful and accurate account of facts, and as such any inattention, use or misuse of the information in question by the reader will render any resulting actions solely under their purview. There are no scenarios in which the publisher or the original author of this work can be in any fashion deemed liable for any hardship or damages that may befall them after undertaking information described herein.

Additionally, the information found on the following pages is intended for informational purposes only and should thus be considered, universal. As befitting its nature, the information presented is without assurance regarding its continued validity or interim quality. Trademarks that mentioned are done without written consent and can in no way be considered an endorsement from the trademark holder.

TABLE OF CONTENTS

INTRODUCTION

Congratulations on purchasing your personal copy of *Debating Alternative Facts: The Elements of Debating and How to Counter Arguments with Ease Using Logic*. Thank you for doing so.

The following chapters will discuss some of the many ways that you can win a debate and how you can make sure that people know the real truth in facts.

You will discover how important it is to always learn the truth and speak it through the debates that you are doing.

The final chapter will explore how to reverse the "logic" of the opposing side and use it to show them that there are real facts.

There are plenty of books on this subject on the market. Thanks again for choosing this one! Every effort was made to ensure it is full of as much useful information as possible. Please enjoy!

CHAPTER 1

The Basics

Throughout history, there have been people who oppose proven facts with nonsense that they either believe in or simply made up. While that element has always been there, there has never been a time more filled with bogus claims than this one. A world where the "leader of the free world" can be a reality show host who has no prior qualifications. Throughout these dark times, you're going to need to know how to debate alternative facts.

Alternative facts, when competing with the official facts, are simply falsifications of opinions or statements by one person or a group of people.

With alternative facts, the extreme right wing of the United States government is able to accomplish anything that they want. Some of the alternative facts that have come about in current events are as follows:

- Smoking doesn't kill people.
- Donald Trump won the election by a landslide.
- Refugees want to come to America to kill.
- Freezing the federal workforce will help the United States' debt crisis.

Throughout each of these "facts," people have reacted and they have simply then been declared as "alternative facts." While we will take a deeper look at each of these facts in a later chapter, you will need to keep in mind that these are all nonsensical claims with no basis of truth to any of them.

The biggest difference between alternative facts and actual facts is truth. Real facts have been proven. There are pictures, videos, studies, and data that have been analyzed, along with information that provides exact proof for the fact. Alternative facts do not have any of that. They are simply an overstated opinion of someone who does not have any qualifications to make that claim. Many times, alternative facts are actually contradicted by other people who are a part of that same party. This is a huge problem, as alternative facts are something that should be consistent throughout all levels of the party. Instead, they are more like a free-for-all for anyone who wants to be able to have them, and use them when it is beneficial to their political views.

If you have ever heard an alternative fact, chances are you may have been taken aback. Just hearing that word can make people balk at the information that they have received and immediately scratch their head at the idea that anyone could believe that so-called fact. The problem, though, is that the people who use alternative facts are usually those who do not have reason.

The real question is, just how do you debate with people who have no reasoning skills?

The answer is complicated. You really cannot debate with the people who believe only in the things that they have made up in their own head, but there are some techniques that you can learn to help you show them what you are talking about. The chances are that they won't change their mind, but you might have a chance at winning the debate if you use the techniques that are outlined in Chapter 10.

As you read through this book, you will be able to recognize some of the elements that you have probably already seen in these "alternative fact-ers," and you will be able to see how they can take your view and turn it around. The book will help you understand how to stand your own ground when it comes to the real facts, what you can do to make sure that you are getting the best principles possible, and the major changes that can be made to better your experience. There are many ways that you can change their minds, just don't let them change yours.

If you have never even had a debate before, or you do not know the right way to do that debate, you will find exactly what you need in this book. You'll learn the right way to debate, the elements of a good debate, and how you can win using some simple facts and techniques that you can combine with powerful methods.

In the following chapter, you will also learn some of the most hotly debated alternative facts. You won't just learn what they are, you will also learn the real facts that go along with them. When you know what the alternative facts are (and what the real facts are), you will then be able to look out for them and figure out if you are really getting the right story.

Not all news outlets are created equal and things like Fox News and CNN have poisoned the minds of many people who want to be able to try new things and make a better decision with the options that they have.

Don't let the news poison your own mind. Know the facts!

CHAPTER 2
Alternative Fact Topics

I f you are going to stand a chance at debating, or even winning the debate on alternative facts, you should know a little bit about each of the alternative facts that some are so fond of. Fighting ignorance with knowledge is one of the best ways that you can win an argument and, hopefully, teach people the things that they need to know about true facts. While this is not necessarily a complete list, these are the most current popular facts. This list includes the alternative facts that are most popular along with the true facts that you will use as your counter argument.

1. Washington D.C. Crime Rates

Donald Trump claimed that the crime rates in Washington, D.C. were steadily rising, and he made the alternative fact statement that it was because of President Obama. In fact, the crime rate saw a decrease in the year 2015.

It decreased by 17% during that time and had seen a huge overall decrease since 1997. The crime rate has been steadily going down since that time, and it is now 55% less than what it was 20 years ago.

2. Media-Invented Intelligence Feud

There is no debating the fact that Trump has a huge feud with the intelligence community. That is one thing he did get right. The alternative fact here is that he says the media invented it, and it just escalated from there. The problem is that Donald Trump took to Twitter to compare intelligence agents to Nazi Germans. There was no media involved in that aspect because he did all of the feuding on his own. Recall the Tweet if alternative fact-ers try to "debate" you on this one.

3. Record Magazine Cover Holder

If this were an official title (and it's not), Donald Trump would try to take it. Trump states that he has been on the cover of Time magazine 15 times in his life. He also says that this is a record because he thinks it seems like a lot of times.

Alternative fact debate #1: Donald Trump has only been on the cover of Time 11 times. Reference their archives for proof.

Alternative fact debate #2: Richard Nixon holds that record (if there even is one) because he was on Time 55 times in his lifetime.

Fun fact: Hillary Clinton has actually been on the cover more times than Trump, and would be closer to the record than him with 22 appearances on that cover.

4. The Huge Crowds at the Inauguration

Inaugurations are usually a pretty big deal when it comes to a new president taking office, so there is really no need to make it seem even bigger than what it was. The Trump backers stated that the crowd was so big it reached the Washington Monument. It didn't though. The proof is in the hundreds of pictures and videos that can be seen during the time of inauguration that simply shows people not reaching back nearly that far.

5. The Inauguration Was the Most Watched

Fan favorite Sean Spicer made note that more people had watched Trump's inauguration than any other president before him. Not true! More people had watched than Obama's inauguration online, but that is where the "more" ends. Around 30 million people watched Trump be sworn into office. In comparison, around 41 million people watched on TV while Ronald Reagan was sworn into office in 1981. Add in the nearly 5 million views that were online (not an option in 1981), and you'll see that it's a little more but not quite enough to compete with that 41 million.

6. First Floor Covering

Trump supporters have claimed that Trump was the first one to use floor coverings during the inauguration. It was a half-baked excuse at why there weren't that many people there or why there appeared to be a lower than average crowd. The problem with that, though, is that at Obama's second inauguration, there were floor backings. The crowd was there, and it didn't appear quite as sparse as it did at Trump's inauguration.

7. Environment Awards

Because he wants so badly to appeal to everyone, Trump made the statement that he "received awards on the environment." The supposed award he got was from creating a nature trail on a golf course that he had broken regulations to build. While it may seem absurd that a president would make a completely false claim (and one that could be easily disproven), it happened. The New Jersey Audubon never gave Trump an award for the golf course or for anything that ever happened on the nature trail with Trump or representatives of.

8. The Media Made Donald Trump Look Bad on Purpose... Again

When the media reported that the head statue of Martin Luther King Jr. had been removed from the White

House, they were receiving false information. The bust is still there, but it was just being covered up by someone who was standing in front of it. When Trump heard that the media reported it as missing, he pointed fingers at them for making it look like he had done something wrong. While trivial, he now refers to the media as liars thanks to this (and many other) instances. To the media, though, it just looked like the bust had been removed. They didn't report it to purposefully make Trump (who was obviously paranoid) look bad.

9. Illegal Votes for Hillary

Perhaps one of the biggest (and worst) alternative facts that were constantly referenced during the election, and even still, is that Hillary had illegal votes going toward her name. While there is almost always some instance of illegal voting going on, there is hardly ever enough to make a difference and, most of the time, it is the individual, not the party, who encourages it.

10. Landslide Victory

Chances are that you have heard that Donald Trump won by a landslide. The problem is, though, that he only won by about a 1% margin. He was actually the 12th closest to not winning the election since we started electing presidents. Donald Trump got 306 votes of the 270 that he needed. For some reason, in his mind, 36 is a really big number and one that qualifies him as a landslide winner. Doing the math, you can see that he wasn't such a big winner.

11. Gunshots and Obama

On January 10th, Barack Obama headed to Chicago to give a farewell speech as the president. He was there giving a good speech (which Trump made sure to make note of), and Trump claimed that, in that time, two people were shot and killed in Chicago.

The problem?

Chicago police have quite a different story. Nobody was shot or killed, as far as they know, on January 10th in Chicago. If Trump isn't getting his information from the police, where did that "fact" come from?

12. Murders in Philadelphia

Donald Trump, even though he lived in New York before moving to D.C., likes to think of Philadelphia as home. Perhaps because that is where he attended college. He mentions that the murder rate in his "home" Philly is "terribly increasing." Again, similar to the D.C. alternative fact that he spouted out, the murder rate is going down. From 2007 to 2016, the murder rate went down by over 120 murders per year. That sounds more like a great decrease.

As any logical person can see, the alternative facts that are included here are completely off the wall and have no basis in reality. The problem, though, is that the people who believe these facts are far from logical and don't really think of anything in terms of reality. They believe what they want to believe, and they don't know what they are talking about most of the time.

If you want any chance of defeating them in a debate, you need to use the information to back up *your* claims. They won't have that same information, so keep that in mind. They don't have proof of any of their claims, so use the "real facts" as proof to help you win the debate. It will also be beneficial for you to know the different aspects of a debate. Help yourself out by being fully prepared to have a debate with someone who may be very far out of touch with reality.

CHAPTER 3
The Elements of a
Good Debate

While it can be really hard to debate with people who are not in touch with reality, there are a few things that you can do that will give you an upper hand. Despite the fact that you are the one who is speaking the truth, you will need to make sure that you are prepared for the debate. One wrong move, and they will jump all over it causing you to lose the debate!

If you want to be able to debate in the best way possible, you should use the elements of a good debate to give yourself have a better chance of winning. Follow this information to make yourself better at debating. It will give you a chance at winning against alternative fact-ers.

The Way You Present

Despite the fact that you are using content to get your point across, it is important that you do what you can to present the case in a professional and appropriate way. You don't want to take digs at the other party on a personal level, and you certainly don't want them to feel like you have insulted them, but you do want to make sure that you show them that there are facts that are real and then there are alternative facts.

If you present in the right way, you will have a better chance at winning the debate. This can be tough to do if you have never debated anything before, but it is a good idea and something that will help you with the debate at hand. Your chances of winning will increase if you present your argument in the right way.

Concise and to the Point

Don't stuff your debate with extra "fluff" and information that will not be helpful to getting your point across. By being concise about the things that you are doing and with the different options you have, you will be able to make it easier to win the debate. You will also allow your true points to stand out among the fluff that the alternative facts are made up of. People who have something to hide or who are not confident about their position will never be able to be concise about it because they don't really know what it is.

Make sure that you are concise with your information and that you are using it to your best advantage. This will help you show off the points that you make and to allow people to see what you are talking about. The concise part of your debate should only be on the facts. When you are done presenting the facts, you can simply stop talking. There is no reason to try to fill in the silence with empty words or fluff that can detract from your statement.

Loudness

The loudness of your voice will have an impact on the debate. Having a loud voice will set you apart as the more dominant person in the equation, and you will be able to get your point across more effectively if you know exactly how loud you need to be to be.

There is a fine line, though. Be careful not to yell or appear like you are screaming at the other person. This will detract from the goals that you have and will make it seem like you are trying too hard to win the debate. Simply raise your voice. Speak firmly and clearly, but do not yell.

The easiest way to figure out the tone that you should use is to consider talking to someone who is on the other side of a room. You wouldn't necessarily yell at them, but you would project your voice far enough that you can make sure that they are able to hear you while you are doing different things.

Be Clear

It can sometimes be hard for people to hear you, especially if they are so focused on their own thoughts and what they are going to respond with. There are many ways that you can get confused during a debate, which can further complicate matters. You should always be clear with what you are saying.

Being clear with your debate not only means that you should enunciate your words and use them in the right context, but it also means that you should not use runaround sentences. Don't keep saying the same thing over and do not talk in circles. That can be confusing for the other party, and it can also be a problem for you because you will simply look like you don't know what you are talking about. When you are clear about your points and the way that you talk about them, you will give yourself a better chance of winning the argument even if it seems impossible.

Case with Content

The content that you present is just as important as the way that you present it. If you are going to be able to win the debate, you will need to make sure that your content is well prepared and well put together so that you don't have to worry about coming up with answers and rebuttals on the spot. Have all of the information that you are going to give your opponent ahead of time and make sure that it is written down.

In your initial presentation, try to think of all of the points that you want to make. It is a good idea to use an outline form to make each of these points so that you can try new things and do more with the initial presentation. Think of all of the things that could come up during the debate and figure out the best way to show your opponent that is what you are talking about. This will help give them a better understanding of what you are talking about and will not waste time by causing them to come up with questions that they think they can use to throw you off.

Rebuttals

The rebuttal period may be the hardest part of the debate. This is because you will need to come up with answers for things that they have stated in somewhat of a question-statement form. There are many different ways that you can choose the rebuttals that you use to answer the questions that they have for you.

Before you even go to the debate, think of all of the things that they may ask you (or if this is a casual debate, just always have the possible questions available). When you do this, think of the way that you are going to answer each of these questions. Is it going to be something that has a concrete answer each time or is it going to be something that will change depending on the context that they ask the question in? No matter what it is that they are planning on asking you, you will always have a rebuttal for what they are saying.

Focus on Methodology

There are many methods that people use to get to logical points, but the idea of people who believe in alternative facts is that they just use the opinions that they have on something and state it as fact. That makes it harder for you to debate with them. Some people just don't want to hear what you have to say. They've already made their mind up and they don't care to change it.

So, instead of focusing on what they are saying and the content, consider stating the fact that they just came up with the idea or that someone somewhere just came up with the idea. This will knock down their ideology because they don't have proof to stand on. Always present the proof that you have for each of the points that you are making. They will soon see all of your points are based on facts, while they have no proof to support them. While it can be difficult to reason with people who don't want to hear it, you will have a better chance at reasoning if you show them that you are truly correct about something because you are actually using facts.

CHAPTER 4
False Equivalency

False equivalency happens when there is an actual fact and when there is an alternative fact. It is a technique that people use to make their alternative facts look similar to the real fact but is actually completely different from the real fact. False equivalency is used a lot by people who want to use alternative facts and who want to compare them to the real facts. It is an important thing for people to look out for if they are debating. Seeing an alternative fact is sometimes difficult for people who are doing debates, and it can be made even more so by the fact that these alternative fact-ers often participate in false equivalency.

Here, we will look at the effects of false equivalency and the way that it is portrayed with modern-day debates. You can learn about many different things when it comes to those situations, but you will also need to learn that it can sometimes be difficult to "turn off" the equivalency theory that alternative facts bring about in their own positions.

Equal but Different

The idea behind equal but different goes all the way back to ancient periods when people were supposed to be equal but were actually treated much differently. The most modern use of the term before today was during the civil rights movements when people were trying to make African Americans feel better about themselves by calling them equal but still managing to treat them different.

The same rings true today with the alternative facts and the information that people are spreading to make things harder on the ones who know the real truth and who are trying to fight the problems that just seem to be getting worse. The idea that the alternative facts are equal, but different, just shows the ignorance level that comes along with the people who believe in them.

There is no such thing as equal but different! It is either equal **or** different, and the people who believe that different things can be equal clearly have no idea what the word truly means.

Change in Equivalency

There will always be some type of change in equivalency when there is a fact and an alternative fact. This can be anything from the changes that happen when there are problems with the way that things are done to the way that things can be made different from the facts that are included with them. If you are careful about what you are doing with your "real" facts, you will be able to make sure that you are using the best experience possible to make it easier to debate the alternative facts.

The equivalence of the alternative facts and the real facts simply does not exist. There is no change in it because it is not something that is real and it can be a problem for the alternative fact-ers who think that they know what they are talking about and that things are able to be different based on their own opinion.

The biggest problem with this is that the people who believe in alternative facts think that their opinions are the same thing as real facts. When they believe that, they think that they can then compare them to the facts and that they will be equal. It brings validation to their opinion and actually has the danger of shaping them to think that they are going to be able to compare what they think to what everyone else knows.

Hillary vs Donald

If you put someone who had graduated from a top school with mediocre grades and a good business history next to someone who had several degrees from Ivy League schools and has an extensive resume of government-based jobs, who do you think would be better qualified to be the president?

There is no denying that Donald Trump is smart in a business sense but that does not mean that he was a good candidate for the presidency. Did he meet all of the qualifications? Yes, but he wasn't even close to as qualified as Hillary Clinton was.

When you look at her resume of political and government-based jobs from an unbiased viewpoint, you can see that she was a better option for the presidency. She knows the different government avenues, she worked as an attorney, and she is the only candidate in history who has had a glimpse inside the private life of a president is really like. The fact that she was the first lady was enough to qualify her alone on the presidency, but it was not something that helped her win.

The fact that Donald and Hillary were essentially compared as equals during the election shows that false equivalency does exist, and it is a real problem in terms of the election that happened in 2016. Donald Trump should never have even been close to comparing to Hillary Clinton. She is far more qualified to be the president than he was or will ever be... even after his four (or, God help us, eight!) years in the White House.

Global Crisis

Alternative fact-ers like to bring up the idea of global

warming. They say that there is no way that it could be happening because of how cold it has been in location X, Y, or Z. They want to bring up the fact that they froze in New England last year or that ice caps are freezing all over the place, but what they fail to realize is that this is an effect of global warming.

Without getting too far into the specific debate of global warming, it is important to note that the false equivalency factor plays into this. It is a false equivalency to think that a colder temperature in any specific region is indicative of there not being any problem with the warming crisis and people should not be really worried about it getting warmer.

This is a complete fallacy because global warming is a real thing. It has been proven by real scientists, and it can be seen at work with different environmental factors. Just because someone can read a thermometer and compare it to last year's temperature doesn't mean that they have proof it isn't happening.

Television Programming

False equivalency is prevalent in television programming all around the United States. The biggest example can be seen with news sources like Fox news. While they are a fear-mongering site that focuses on people who don't have a lot of education and who believe in alternative facts, they are consistently being compared to some of the true, big name news outlets. This is a huge problem because people think that just because Fox says something that is opposite of one of the more fact-based news outlets that it is equal to what they are saying in real news. It is not though. There are no facts that are on Fox, and that is a huge problem for people who want to get the real news but who may not know that Fox is fake.

It is important to understand that alternative fact-ers are the ones who want to buy into the news on Fox. They follow these fake news sources, and they try to make facts out of them. This is where the idea that they do not just have an opinion comes from. They think that because they saw it on a news channel, even if it is Fox, it is true and it is fact.

Rights for Women

One major problem that comes with false equivalency is rights for women. Alternative fact-ers show that women are making more money than they ever have before and they even have the right to vote. True fact-ers know that while women are making more money than in the past, they are still not making as much as men and they are having their rights stripped from them on a regular basis by the Republicans.

Women are not equal to men in the world that we live in, but the alternative fact-ers want people to think that they are.

Protecting LGBTQ

Throughout the past 10 years, there have been huge strides made for the LGBTQ community. Now, those are at risk because of false equivalency. Those who believe in the alternative facts think that just because everyone has the right to marry means that they are equal. This is not the case and is a huge problem for the LGBTQ community. They are treated with disrespect; private businesses regularly turn them away in the Bible Belt, and many people still look at them differently. False equivalency runs rampant when it comes to LGBTQ and the rights that they have.

CHAPTER 5
Facts vs Opinions

When you are dealing with alternative facts and the people who believe in them, you will need to have a clear understanding of what a fact is. You should also know a lot about what an opinion is because that is something that most alternative facts really are. If you know what both of these things are and you are able to define them while fitting different things into their categories, you will be able to make the right decision on what a fact and an opinion are. This will not only help you to differentiate the alternative facts in your daily life, but it will also give you a chance to see what the difference is in a real debate.

Basic Ideas

A fact is something that is able to be proven. It has to have some type of method that can prove it to be able to be considered a fact, and it must be something that is based in truth. An opinion, on the other hand, may be possible to prove but doesn't have to be. At its core, an opinion is really just a free-for-all to someone who wants to believe different things.

A fact is a known piece of information that can be used for different purposes. An opinion is something that someone just thinks.

Facts

If you are looking at a piece of information and someone has something that will prove it, then it is a fact. The information that proves that it is real makes it a fact. Until someone is able to produce information that will discredit it as a fact, it will remain a fact, and it will be considered the truth that people need to be able to hear.

Here are some examples of facts and how they are proven:

- The grass is green – when you look at a piece of grass compared to something that is not green, you can see that the grass is green .
- Humans are alive – you can see humans move, breathe, and do different life processes. It is a fact that they are alive.
- Hillary Clinton is qualified to be the president – she meets the minimum qualifications, and she has real experience and true education that she has worked on to make her qualified. It is a fact.

- Planes fly – planes that are up in the air and are moving in any direction are flying. The fact shows only that they are able to be in the air and fly.
- Cars cause smog, which hurts the environment – the cars that are on the road have a negative effect on the environment. It has been proven that smog is not good for cities or even entire regions because of the way that they are able to be positioned in different areas.

Opinions

An opinion is just a bit more complicated than a fact. It is something that someone believes. They can either base their beliefs off of something that is a real and true fact, or they can choose different methods for their beliefs. An opinion is neither right nor wrong on its own, but when it goes against a fact, it is wrong. If you see a pattern here, that is because alternative facts go against facts. They are just opinions. What is even worse about that fact is that they are wrong opinions because they go against information that has been proven as a fact.

Even if the majority of people accept an opinion as something that they all believe in, that does not make it a fact. It simply makes it a widely accepted opinion that has gained mass support and is able to change the minds of people despite the fact that it may or may not be true.

Keep in mind that some opinions can turn into facts. All facts started out as opinions, and then, they were changed into facts when you are able to prove them. All facts were once opinions, but not all opinions are going to turn into facts.

Here are some examples of opinions that may look similar to facts:

- The grass is always green – this is not the case. While grass is green when it is alive and in most instances, it is, it can be other colors. There are varieties of grass that can be purple and even red. Some grass is brown because it is dead. In the winter, grass doesn't go away, but it does turn brown.

- Humans know how to live – humans don't know how to live when they are first born. While everyone has survival skills, they must be taught different ways to not die while they are young. Further, some humans do not have a very enjoyable life, and people may say that they are not living their life.

- Hillary Clinton should have been the president – as much as this is a widely accepted opinion by those who do not believe in alternative facts and who are based in reality, it is still just an opinion. Despite the fact that she did have all of the qualifications, the only way to say that she should have been president is through opinion. To make this a factual statement, you would need to come up with real, viable proof that she lost unfairly (through the use of deceptive methods or other problems with the election). Despite the fact that you think that she should have won as do many people, this is an opinion.

- Planes are fun – the planes that are in the air are flying. The planes that are in the air are safe. This is because they have been proven to be both flying through the air and exhibiting certain levels of safety while they are doing so. The safety of planes has been proven over and over again (ask any anxious flyer). There are many people who think that planes are fun, but this is just their opinion. The idea of fun is something that depends on different people. Flying can be fun for person 1, but for person 2, flying can be a miserable experience that they avoid at all costs despite the fact that it is still safe.

- Cars that cause smog make a city ugly – most people would agree that smog is ugly and is not something that they would want to look at on a regular basis because of the way that it changes things and makes them look bad, but that is just an opinion. There is a chance that someone out there thinks that smog is pretty, and they like to look at it over cities and in areas that they are at. The smog is still bad for the city, which is a fact, but the people may think that it looks nice.

When looking at all of these examples and the similarities that lie between them, you can clearly see how it can be confusing to get facts and opinions mixed up. This may be one of the reasons why people still believe in alternative facts. They are being fed these "alternative facts" in the form of fact when they are actually opinions. The people may not know better, but the greater chance is that the people have simply chosen to ignore the fact that alternative facts are nothing more than opinions because they are the same opinions that they have and they want to have something that lines up with their own beliefs. Because of this, the opinion grows into an even bigger alternative fact and then, soon, everyone believes it.

Another tactic that people use with facts and opinions is emotional language. They spin facts or opinions around and make them seem like they are a question instead of the statement that they are. If you are looking at the facts as a question, it may be harder for you to determine whether or not they are real or they are just something that you think you have heard. This is because it connects with your emotional side, and you could start to question it because of the implications that it has on your emotions.

News outlets, like Fox, choose to do the opposite of that. They portray the opinions in such a way that people think they are facts. They talk about them as if they were facts, or they will say words that make them seem like facts. Because of regulations of the news, they cannot say that something is a fact when it is actually an opinion, but there is no regulation on the way that they say things. When they are looking at different things in context, it will mean different things, and they could change the context of an opinion to make it a fact, which is how alternative facts start out.

CHAPTER 6
Objective and Subjective During Debates

There are two main types of mindsets that people who are debating have. One person always has an objective frame of mind and the other subjective. Not only are people able to be subjective, but entire organizations and even news outlets are subjective as well. In general, news outlets should be objective so that people do not get the wrong idea or they do not have to worry about the problems that come from something that is based on opinion or personal experiences, but that does not matter to some news outlets.

Objective and Subjective

In nearly all situations, there is a party that is subjective while there is also a party who is objective. The subjective party is usually much less reasonable than the objective party, and that is something that creates major waves in debates and other situations. If you are having a debate with someone and you are trying to be objective, the chances are that they are subjective and do not even know it.

Being subjective means that someone is not very open minded about anything. They have their opinions, and they use them instead of facts. They base nearly everything off of the emotions that they feel and the way that they think that things should be done. In general, people who believe in alternative facts are those who are subjective, and that can make it hard to reason with them. Instead of reasoning, they use their emotions. They don't do anything to back up their own claims, and they struggle to touch base with reality no matter what situation they are in.

Objective as a Whole

If you have a perspective that you don't think is influenced by anything inside or out aside from the facts, the chances are that you are objective. This can be difficult for some people to understand, but it is a way of thinking that all people are able to adapt to if they work hard enough. You may have beliefs, but they are not influenced by the things that you think or the things that other people think.

Objective people and organizations do not let emotions or opinions play into the perspective that they have on things. They are able to mute their personal feelings about things too, which makes it much easier for them to look at something in a neutral way. Because of the way that objective people are able to do different things and have an understanding of those things, they are much better at understanding information and processing it to use for debates. Objective people are easier to reason with and often have a much more open mind than those who are subjective and let their emotions get in the way of things that they see in their lives and all around them.

Subjective as a Whole

People who have subjective viewpoints tend to not take many different things into account. They are subject to the opinions and the feelings that the person or the organization has because they do not have a very open mind. When someone is subjective, they are only able to look on the inside and they don't know what to look for on the outside. If someone is subjective about something, the chances are that they don't have a very open mind and are not willing to look at things from the other perspectives that are available. It is their way or no way as far as they are concerned.

The majority of people who are subjective will be somewhat uneducated and will not have a huge worldview. This can be a problem because of the way that they do things. Even though they think that they are right about everything, they don't have the experience that is needed to show people that they are right. They certainly don't turn to facts or proof to back them up. They will often use things like *I think* and *they said* to get their point across. If someone is subjective, it can be hard to reason with them.

People Who are Subjective

The majority of people who believe in alternative facts are those who are subjective. This is because of the problems that they have with accepting reality and because of the way that they do different things. It is something that they may not know about and something that they will have to deal with because they have chosen that path. It is hard for them, though, to try and find new things that are related to the different options that they are going up against.

If someone is subjective, you will likely struggle to reason with them because of the facts that they believe in. These facts are really just opinions, but they have the feeling that if someone else has stated them then they must be right, too. The ideas that they have are often not their own and are really just based on what others have told them to believe and what they think is the truth. If you want to make sure that you are truly helping people to understand what alternative facts are (opinions), you will need to recognize that they are not even able to think for themselves.

When News Is Subjective

Perhaps one of the worst things about subjective ways of

thinking is that many people who think in a subjective perspective are able to all gather together and try to come up with ideas. Those ideas just turn into everyone's opinions. Because of the way that subjective people think, they believe that they are all right because they all have the same beliefs. This is what leads to entire organizations, like news networks, that are reporting false information based on alternative facts. Just because more than one person believes something is true does not make it true. News outlets like Fox news like to give out information that is incorrect and is really just a whole lot of opinions jumbled together.

It is important to note that news that is subjective should never be listened to or taken into account. Subjective news sources have the right to give the things that they think are true, but they have to be careful about how they word it. To a regular person, it is difficult to tell the difference in all of the things that are true or not true. If you want to figure out what type of news source is real, always look for one that is objective and not subject to what other people have to say or the opinions of people who think they know what they are doing.

Idea Behind Objective

The ideas that are behind objectives are that people are able to look at things as if they were an object instead of with emotions and feelings tied to them. Their perspective is nothing more than a way to look at things and the results that come from them. If you are using perspective to look at different options, it is not something that you will be able to figure out using your own emotions and the feelings that you get from things.

Objective reasoning is all about how far away you can step from your feelings and the opinions that other people have. If you know what you are doing, all you need to do is look at something as if it had no effect on your emotion. Even when things do affect your emotions, you will need to get rid of those emotions and use the objective point of view to discover something. It can be hard to do, but it will be worth it in the end when you are more logical than those who are subjective with their view of the world.

Errors from Subjective Outlook

There are so many errors that can come from having a subjective outlook on life. This is because of all of the problems that are associated with being subjective, and it is something that can cause even more problems for people who are in different situations. This is a major issue for things like news networks and entire political parties.

One person who is hugely subjective and now has a cult-like following that is similarly subjective is Donald Trump.

He bases his "alternative facts" off of things that he has heard and knows just a little about. He gets angry easily when things are different from what he is used to, and that can cause problems with the way that things are now done in the government. When Donald Trump entered the White House, so did an era of people who can't think for themselves, let their emotions cloud their vision, and have no idea how to open their minds to things that are new to them.

The United States is in the age of being subjective and it is important that you try to remain objective during these difficult times.

CHAPTER 7

Understanding an Opposing View

Everyone has viewpoints. That is how they get their opinion across and how they are able to show people what they are talking about. When someone has a viewpoint that they are trying to figure out, they will need to make sure that they have an understanding of the way that the opposing view works. It is something that can be complicated, but if you know what you are doing, it will be much easier for you to make the decision on how you are going to understand their viewpoint.

Hearing the Point of View

The first part of learning and understanding what someone is talking about and their point of view is to hear them out. There is more to listening than just taking information in, so you should make sure that you are actually comprehending their point of view.

It is necessary for you to take a break and listen to what the person who is on your opposing side is trying to say. Even if you don't think that it is a good point or that they are wrong, the listening part is necessary. You may find that you will learn during this time why they believe in alternative facts or what has made them want to be able to figure out what they are doing things for. It is a good idea to try and make sure that you are listening to them so that they will know what you are talking about when it is your turn. You will want to include information about things that they said and use your reasoning as to why it is completely wrong.

Understanding What It Means

Do not have a goal of responding as soon as you know what they are talking about. Instead, listen so that you can understand what the opposing side is saying. The understanding that you get from them being able to get their point across and from making sure that you can get the most out of the points that they are talking about is something that will help you to have a better understanding of what is going on in their side of the debate.

You can understand what they are saying by stopping and listening. Consider writing down the points that they are making so that if you have questions, later on, you can ask them. It is also a good idea while you are writing things down to write how it pertains to the information that you are going to be able to use to make your experiences better. The information that you use will determine the way that you can do things and how it will make your part of the debate go much more smoothly.

Breaking It Down

This can be the hardest part of the debate process especially when you are dealing with people who believe in alternative facts. The breakdown process should involve looking at the way that they think, the things that they are doing, and the way that you can make sure that you are learning from them. Take apart the things that they are talking about and use them to your advantage so that you can figure them out and apply them.

Similar to how you broke your own thoughts down into sections when you were preparing your debate, you can break their argument into smaller sections. This can be made up of the information that is used in the debate along with all of the other things that they are saying. You may want to consider writing down what is true and what is just speculation. This will help you to separate their alternative facts from the true facts that you are using in different instances. When you want to be able to use the facts to your advantage, you will know what facts are going to go against the true facts that you have already lined up for your own argument.

Dissecting the Information

Once you have the information, it is broken down into different categories and you know what you are going to use it for, you can dissect the information and combine it with different things so that you will know what you are going to be able to do with it. This is something that can be beneficial to your experiences and something that will help to strengthen your argument.

One of the biggest benefits that come from dissecting the information that the opposing side has created is that you will then be able to insert snippets of it into your debate. You will, obviously, not be using the alternative facts, but you can pick up on the language that was used and some of the information that was being talked about for different verification purposes. Simply try to make sure that you are going to be able to use that information to your own benefit and draw it into your own debate.

Even though the chances are that your debate has already been written and you know what you are talking about, you will still be able to put some of that information into your debate.

Making the Determination

This is the single most important part of the debate that you will use. It is necessary for you to try and make sure that you are going to be able to put different things into play and be able to add additional information to your part of the debate. If you don't know what hard facts and alternative facts are from the other side's debate, you aren't going to be able to use that to your own advantage. Try to make sure that you are doing what you can so that you can make sure that you are not going to be using their alternative facts. You will look like a fool if you are trying to debunk their alternative facts and end up using them in your own argument.

This is also the point that you will determine what alternative facts they are talking about and what you are going to debate against. You can simply jot down the different things that they are talking about and try to make that determination when it comes to the different things that you are doing. This can be difficult as the debates usually go quickly, so make sure that you are prepared to determine what you are going to make note of in their debate.

Clarifying for Fallacies

The chances are that you are going to need to ask some questions or try to figure out what they are talking about when it comes to different subjects that they are debating. This can sometimes be difficult depending on what you are doing and what you want to be able to do, so make sure that you are doing everything that you can to get to the bottom of their argument.

You will need to clarify what they are talking about and the alternative facts that they are using if you want to be able to weed out any fallacies that are present in their argument. It is necessary to show them that they are not talking about anything that is beneficial or anything that is truly the way that it is supposed to be. By doing this, you will guarantee that you are going to win the argument. Once you can prove what they are talking about is a complete untruth, you will then be able to show them that you are right and the debate will be over.

Looking at It Objectively

The other side is always going to be subjective if they are using alternative facts. That is because they do not know how to think for themselves and they do not know the right way to be able to come up with their own facts. Because of this, you are going to have to be the objective party in the debate. You need to look at the whole argument in an objective sense and then use that to your advantage. When you can listen to what they are saying and not have an emotional response to it, you will be much better off with the goals that you have. You will also be able to win the debate.

It can sometimes be difficult if you have not ever been in a debate with someone who is very subjective, but being as objective as much as possible can help you to win the debate. The chances are that you will even teach the person who you are debating the right way to be objective and how they can overcome the emotional feelings that they get when they are doing different things or reacting to different information that is present in the argument they are making.

CHAPTER 8
Strategies for Debating

Despite the fact that you may have a really good argument that you are going to make to the person who believes in alternative facts, you will still need to use some strategies for debate that will help you to win the debate. This is especially true when you are unable to reason with people because you won't be able to win just by showing them the logical truth. Always use these strategies when you are debating alternative facts so that you can be sure that you will win. Some strategies are commonly recognized while others are swept under the rug for being morally questionable. Keep all of that in mind when you are using them and decide which ones you are comfortable with using.

Double Speak

This way of talking is something that you can use during the debate to show that you are just repeating what you have said before. Some people liken it to talking in circles while others see it as a way to get your point across more effectively.

If you are going to use double speak, you will need to make sure that you are prepared for it. Otherwise, your points could seem invalid and that could cause problems if you want to be able to win the debate that you are participating in. The biggest problem that comes with double speak is that you may not know what you are doing with it or you may run into problems that will cause you to have trouble using your own information.

Double speak is a fan favorite of many right-wing conservatives so make sure that you are aware of that when you are just getting started with the debate. Look out for someone who may be trying to double speak debate you.

Cue Cards

While this is more of a helpful tip instead of an actual strategy, you can use cue cards that will help you to figure out what you are talking about. There are some things that you will need to remember when using cue cards:

- Don't write out the entire debate – just a few key points.
- Make sure that you keep them to a minimum.
- Avoid reading directly from the cue card; instead, use it to get yourself acquainted with the ideas that come

from the cue cards. This will help you to figure out the right way to do things with your debate and what you want to be talking about.

- Try to avoid shuffling the cue cards or moving them around; this may happen when you are nervous, but it can detract from your argument.

There are many different things that go into using cue cards, but be sure that you are prepared for them. Even some of the best attorneys and people who debate still use cue cards, so it is clear that they can be very helpful if you use them the right way in your debate.

Complex Vocabulary

By using a complex vocabulary, you will be able to make changes to the way that you are talking and to the information that you are using. This can sometimes confuse the other party. It is not a good idea to try and win a debate based solely on the confusion of the other party, but it is something that you can use to help confuse them and to make things harder for them to grasp the concept of.

Using a complex vocabulary when you are debating with people who believe in alternative facts is especially helpful. The majority of the time, the people who you are debating with are not very intelligent, and the vocabulary that you use will likely be enough to leave them flustered after you have presented your argument. Just be sure that you are using the vocabulary in the right way. If you get caught using words that don't mean what you think they mean or using words out of context, you will end up being the one side of the debate that looks ignorant. Study up and learn the right words to use to help you get a better idea of what you are doing.

Deflection

When someone says a point, you can redirect it back to them and use the power of deflection to help yourself win the debate. This is a good idea if you want to make sure that you are using it the right way and if you want to be able to try new things in the debate areas that you are using. It is especially important if the person is completely unreasonable with the points that they have made.

A good example of deflection is simply stating the fact back to them but using it in a different context. If you can show them that what they are saying is ridiculous, then you are conquering deflection. It will help you to have a better understanding of the right way to win a debate and what you can do to make your debate go more smoothly. There are many different things that go into deflection, so keep that in mind while you are debating and what you are going to use. You may find that deflection is extremely helpful to you and that you will be able to use it in the best way possible.

Always remember to point their argument back at them. When they see it from an outside point of view, they may recognize just how ridiculous it is.

Assumptions

If the opposing party does not make their point clear with anything that they are talking about, the only thing that you can do is assume what they mean. This can sometimes be difficult for people to understand, and some may think of it in a way that might not line up with what they believe in morally, but the fact is that when someone who is debating does not state their point or make it clear to anyone else, they are leaving themselves open to interpretation, which often means that someone else can assume what they mean.

On the contrary, make sure that you do not leave yourself open to assumptions. Doing so could compromise your argument and could really hurt your chances of being able to win the debate. If there is anything that someone might be able to assume the position that you hold for your debate, you need to make sure that you clarify it and try to do something else. The clarification process will allow you the chance to show other people that you really mean what you say and care about what you are saying.

Definitions of Concepts

Defining the concepts that other people are doing is a great way to ensure that you are going to be able to use the elements to your advantage. The way that you define their concepts is to simply ask them what they mean. If they state that they think that something is "bad," find out what bad means to them and how they define the idea behind bad. Doing this will not only help you to get a clearer picture of the concepts that they are talking about, but it will also help to wear them down when it comes to the information that they are talking to you about.

Some people may find that they are struggling to get the exact definition that they need. This can be a problem when it comes to the different options that you have and when you are going to be able to use this information for yourself. By looking at the different aspects of a debate and defining each of the concepts that your opponent is talking about, you will help yourself to be fully prepared to present your argument and show them what you are talking about. Always remember to define your own concepts in your argument.

Additional Elements

There is always a way to add additional elements to your argument. This can mean that you are putting more information in, you are adding different things to the argument, or you are working to try new things with the arguments that you are making. It is necessary if you are going to try and confuse your opponent.

The idea behind adding additional elements is that you will be able to fluster them and to confuse them to the point where they are no longer able to logically talk about their point. Doing this is a great way to help yourself win and will give you a chance at doing better with the debate that you have. It will also help you to win against opponents who seem to be relatively unreasonable. There are many ways that you can do this, and that will help you to get more information that you need while also securing your position as the winner of the debate.

Not all of these strategies will guarantee a win, and you should not use them all at one time, but they will help you to have a better time at the debate. You will make your argument easier on yourself, and you'll be able to show you opponent what you are talking about even if they are not being logical about things.

CHAPTER 9
How Statistics Can Be Manipulated

When you are looking at statistics, it is easy to see that they are concrete evidence that you can use as proof of the argument that you are making. The problem with statistics, though, is that they can be very easily manipulated. This means that you may not be able to really get the whole truth when it comes to the statistics that you are hearing about while you are in the midst of a debate. Since statistics are an important part of any type of debate, you will need to make sure that you know how they can be manipulated and what you can do about them.

The Statistics That Are Chosen

Each time that someone wants to use statistics for a debate, they can choose the ones that they want to be able to use. That is one of the biggest problems with statistics in debates. You do not have to use all of the statistics that are included on a certain subject. In general, those who are debating may choose a statistic because of the following:

- It further strengthens their own point.
- It makes the other party's point seem invalid.
- It seems like it could be factual even when it is dissected and only parts of it are used.
- It was something that helped them to have an understanding of what they were talking about and what they believe in.

When a statistic lines up with what someone believes in or what they want to get their point across about, they will almost always use that exact statistic in the argument that they are making. You should keep this in mind when you are doing different things and when you are listening to the various arguments that are provided by people who are in different areas of their own argument. If you do not think that the statistic is going to help the cause, simply do not listen to it and do not use it to make yourself have a better understanding of the way that the argument is going.

It can sometimes be hard to be able to get what you need out of the different statistics. This is true even when you are using statistics for your own argument. Keep that in mind and only use statistics that you think will work in your favor. Choose wisely so that you can make sure that you are using ones that contribute to your cause.

For example, if you are trying to get your point across about murder rates and crime rates that are decreasing, only use statistics from cities where they are actually decreasing. Don't use statistics from cities where the crime rates are going up or staying the same; that would not help your argument.

The Way They Are Presented

As with all things in a debate, the way that you present your statistics is going to have a huge impact on the way that they are used. If you know the right way to present them and to show the other party the truth about the facts that you are stating, you will need to make sure that you present them in a positive light. Even if the statistics are not all positive, presenting them in that way will give you a chance to be able to try new things and to show off the knowledge that you have of the different parts of the subject that you are talking about. It can sometimes be intimidating to know that you are the only one responsible for the education of the facts, but by keeping that in mind, you will give yourself a better chance at winning the argument and being able to conquer the debate that you are having.

Keep in mind that the other party is also going to be presenting the facts that they believe in (the alternative facts) and that they are going to use them to their advantage. If you know what you are doing, you will be able to overcome those facts though, and the statistics for those will not matter even though they are trying to manipulate you by using the statistics.

One of the biggest supporters of presenting statistics for manipulation in a debate is Donald Trump. He and his party often use a lot of statistics that may not be correct, but they are presented in a way that makes people who do not know any better believe them. When Donald Trump talked about the murder rates in Philadelphia rising in the past 10 years, he didn't actually include any factual information. In fact, this was a statistic that he had pulled from someone else who was misinformed, and he used it to his own benefit. This is a huge problem because then he caused thousands of people to have that same belief when it wasn't, in fact, true at all. Donald Trump presents false statistics in a way that makes them look like they are real, and that is how the idea of alternative facts being used in his campaign really started.

Always try to make sure that you are using statistics that are true. Even if you have to present them in a way that makes them look better, they should have some basis in truth. That is one of the hallmarks of a good debater because they know that they are able to use truth and just present it in the right way to win. If you do use things that are false and you try to present them in a way that makes them look real, then you won't have a chance to be able to understand what you are doing and the way that things are going to go for your debate. Always be truthful, no matter how you have to present that truth.

Always Question

Now that you know the right way to be able to use the truth in your own debate, you need to understand what has to be done when you come up against someone who is not using the truth in the debate that they are doing. This can be difficult because these people will use anything that they can to make them look better – even if it means making up fake statistics and presenting them in a way that looks truthful!

The chances are that, if you hear a fake statistic, you will be able to recognize that there might be something wrong with that statistic. During a debate, you are absolutely allowed to ask questions if you want to find out where the information came from. In some instances, you may need to stop the person from presenting and simply ask them where the statistical information came from. If they do not have a response to where it came from, if they tell you that they don't know, or if they make up a new source or use one that is completely based on falsified information, you will know that the statistic is fake.

Asking questions about the statistic is what can actually help you to win the argument. Until you ask where the person got their information from, you could be losing the argument. You might not even be able to do anything about the argument that is happening, but as soon as they cannot produce credible information about the statistic that they used, you will seal the deal for winning. As soon as someone lets you know that they are not doing something in the way that they should be or that they are not using the information appropriately or if it is not based in truth, they won't really be able to argue their point anymore because they will know that they have been found out about the fake information that they are using.

Always keep this in mind when you are debating and when someone uses something that you think is fake. Whether it is statistics, information that they are providing, or "proof" that they are using, question them about it. The chances are that they are bluffing and were just hoping that you wouldn't ask them to see where it came from.

The chances of winning are good after you have exposed statistical manipulation. If you can do it, always try to make sure that is what you are going to do to win the argument. While there are different ways to win the argument, exposing fake statistics is almost completely guaranteed to show your opponent that you are going to win. It will help you to have a better experience when it comes to the information that you are using to your own benefit and with the different options that are included in your experiences.

CHAPTER 10
Using Your Opponent's Argument Against Them

For years, people have been debating. For those same years, people have been losing debates because their own argument was used against them. This is a technique that can be easily used to make sure that people are able to win debates. If you want to win the debate that you are having with an alternative fact-er, you will need to know exactly how to use their argument against them. Since there are several different ways to do this, you need to look at all of your different options and figure out which one is going to be the best for you to use.

Find a Weakness

Every argument is going to have some sort of weakness to it. Whether it is with the statistics that are not real, the lack of proof for the argument, or the information is simply incorrect, you will be able to find a weakness in your opponent's argument if you just listen to the argument and try to pick out where they are faltering.

One of the ways that you can spot a weakness is listening to the way that they talk. If they get quiet during a certain part of their argument, if they speak faster than they had been, or if they falter with their words, the chances are that those may be the weak spot of the argument. Use that to your advantage and try to make sure that you are going to be able to use it against them while you are doing different things with the arguments that they have and that they are talking about. It can sometimes be complicated to figure out exactly what they are talking about, so try to keep that in mind while you are looking at the different aspects of their argument and with what you have to hear about the argument.

Turn Around the Argument

Once you are able to listen to it, comprehend it and know the weak spots, turn the argument around on them. Bring up the weak points that you know they have in the argument since you looked for the clues for it and since you know what you are going to do with that type of argument. You should also simply flip the argument and start arguing back with their own points. There is a good chance that they will see the errors of their ways and that they will be able to recognize that they have a terrible platform to stand on if they are not using the information in the correct way.

Try to figure out what you want to be able to show them or teach them with their own argument. If you know this, you will have a much easier time turning it around on them. You will, obviously, want to show them that your side is right but consider how it relates to their argument and make note of that. If you can turn their argument into something that is close to what you are doing then you will be closer to winning the debate that you are a part of.

Show Them Opposite Statistics

The chances are that your opponent is using fake statistics or is simply manipulating the statistics so that they suit his or her needs. This is a major problem with debates and something that you need to consider while you are debating. If you want to be able to try new things with your debates and with what you have to offer, just show them the opposite statistics to what they are talking about.

This can be difficult to do, so keep that in mind while you are trying new things and when you want to be able to use more statistics to your advantage. As you learn more about the statistics that you have, you will be able to try new things and to make sure that you are letting them see that their statistics are really just outrageous. They may not get what you are trying to do, but they will certainly recognize their own statistics and will see that there is a major problem with what they are talking about.

If you are going to show them statistics that are the polar opposite of what they are talking about, make sure that you are clear on that point and that you do what you can to let them know that they are wrong!

Be Quiet

Once they have finished their argument, be quiet for a few minutes. This is a psychological technique. When someone is talking to someone or trying to get their point across and the person does not respond, they will feel the need to keep talking. This can help you because they will often talk even more about what they don't know anything about and what is wrong information. This will make them look like even more of a fool and can cause major problems with the basis of their argument.

It is always a good idea to try more and to do more, but sometimes doing nothing is the only thing that you need to do while you are in the midst of a debate. The next time that you are talking to someone in an ordinary conversation, try this technique. The chances are that they will keep talking and adding information if you don't respond.

Ask Them to Consider

This is something that you can do to change their views and use their argument against them (and in your favor). Simply ask them to consider for a few moments what they are talking about. They may stop and take inventory of what they are saying and how that can mean negative effects for them. If they do this, the chances are that they will see that they were erroneous in their beliefs and that they will need to change their point of argument. Sometimes, though, this does not work, but while they are considering their argument, it will buy you some time to come up with more points as to why they are wrong.

It is not always the best decision to trick the person who you are debating with, but that is sometimes the only choice that you have. This is especially true when you are in a debate with someone who believes in alternative facts, so keep that in mind the next time that you try to debate with them. The only way that some of them will listen is if you turn their own basis for a debate around on them and show them that the things that they have been thinking of are not quite what they seemed before.

CONCLUSION

Thank for making it through to the end of *Debating Alternative Facts: The Elements of Debating and How to Counter Arguments with Ease Using Logic.* Let's hope it was informative and able to provide you with all of the tools you need to achieve your goals of winning a debate against someone who believes in alternative facts. Even if it does feel impossible, you will have the tools and the know-how that you need to make sure that you are going to be able to beat them and teach them the truth about real facts.

The next step is to try and make sure that you are creating your own argument based on the real facts that have been proven to be true. You will also need to study up on some of the arguments that they use so that you can be sure you are prepared to win that debate.

Finally, if you found this book useful in any way, a review on Amazon is always appreciated!

www.ingramcontent.com/pod-product-compliance
Lightning Source LLC
Chambersburg PA
CBHW070931280326
41934CB00009B/1836